# THE WORLD'S CRAZIEST COURT CASES

ROSEMARY FURBER

Crombie Jardine
PUBLISHING LIMITED
Office 2, 3 Edgar Buildings
George Street
Bath
BA1 2FJ
www.crombiejardine.com



First published by
Crombie Jardine Publishing Limited, 2006



ISBN 1-905102-92-5 (10-digit)
ISBN 978-1-905102-92-1 (13-digit)

Written by Rosemary Furber
Edited by Christine Rista
Designed by www.glensaville.com

Printed and bound in Great Britain by
William Clowes Ltd, Beccles, Suffolk

People will sue for the craziest reasons. You only have to read this collection of weird and wonderful – but true – court cases to understand the origins of that well-known saying:

**If you can smile in adversity, you've thought of somebody you can sue.**

# CONTENTS

# NICE WORK!

At the international accountancy firm Deloittes, getting the staff to walk across burning embers barefoot was just another day at the office. The fire walk was part of a course to prove that accountants could do the impossible, and had been used plenty of times before. Unfortunately this time, one senior accountant had had a pedicure a few days before, and the soles of her feet were extra-sensitive to 'fire-kisses'. The firm was fined £3,000 plus costs.

Smoking can be more dangerous than one thinks. On 13 July 2003 John Jenkins sat down in a portable loo in Tennessee and to aid the cogitative process, he lit a cigarette. The toilet exploded. Methane was leaking from a broken pipe underneath the portable loo. *(Dominion-Post, West Virginia)*

# NICE WORK!

Employees in California won $172 million in a class action against Wal-Mart for making them work too hard. They claimed they had been 'brainwashed' into accepting unfeasible deadlines and had had to work through their lunch and tea breaks, without pay, to meet them. Worst of all, they had been forced to sing the Wal-Mart song during almost every shift. *(Associated Press, 2001 & Times, 23 December 2005)*

# I SUE YOU!

Deputy head teacher Sue Storer sued her school in Bristol for making her sit in an embarrassing chair. Her joint deputies, both men, were bought new, silent chairs while she and her 'farting chair' were the butt of everybody's jokes. A tribunal dismissed her £1 million claim; she should have bought a new chair herself. *(Times, 10 April 2006)*

# NICE WORK!

Raymond Akers, 52, was tired of being restricted at the office. His female colleagues could wear skimpy outfits which he felt were not 'business-like', whilst he had to wear boring ties. So one day he turned up in one festooned with pictures of brightly coloured condoms. The tribunal told him not to be 'silly' and, no, they did not want to see the tie in question. *(Times, 3 June 2006)*

# I SUE YOU!

In Memphis, Brian Delekta is suing his school for not giving him A+ in an exam. He came top of his class with an A+ in 2002 and says that the A he got in the following year was unjust. The school principal and seven school board members named as defendants should all have done better. *(CBS News, 6 February 2003)*

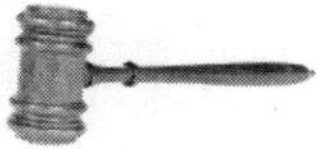

# NICE WORK!

Ohio State University officials closed off streets and called in the bomb squad when a sticker was spotted on a bike saying 'This Bike is a Pipe Bomb'. The bike's owner, 28 year-old Patrick Hanlin, was charged with inducing panic. No bomb was found, and it was explained that 'This Bike is a Pipe Bomb' is the name of a punk rock band, from Pensacola, Florida. *(Columbus Dispatch, Ohio, 5 April 2006)*

# I SUE YOU!

Do you want to speak to the man in charge or the woman who knows what's going on? An accounts clerk in Greenwich, Connecticut, is suing her boss for $28,700 worth of overtime, which she claims she's had to put in to cover up her boss's 11-year affair. If she loses, she'll set his mobile phone to stun. *(Anne Frank v Dept of Parks and Recreation of Greenwich, 2003)*

# NICE WORK!

Are people who are late more fun than the people who wait for them? A California jury thought not. To show how to treat someone who's late for a meeting, an 'Alarm One' boss made 53 year-old Janet Orlando bend over in front of her young colleagues, mostly male, while he paddled her with a metal sign. She won $1.7 million damages. How about a spanking new job, Ms Orlando? Don't need one, thanks. *(Reuters, 29 April 2006)*

# I SUE YOU!

In a Connecticut Court side room, attorney Milo J Altschuler wanted to make sure his client gave the right answers in the witness box so he put her across his lap and slapped her buttocks. He had threatened other clients with this treatment before, to make sure they were more frightened of him than of cross-examination. His American Home Insurance policy was held not to apply: 'fondling the bare bottoms of female clients ... is not part of the practice of law.' *(Law.com, 15 July 2002)*

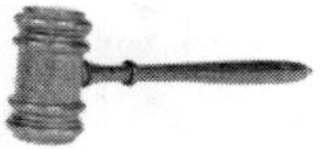

# NICE WORK!

A young barrister claimed that her unpaid pupilage was an employment contract under the National Minimum Wage Act 1998, so wasn't it about time somebody paid her some money? The wolf was at her door and he was bringing his own sandwiches. The Court of Appeal said that she did have a contract, and her work was valuable, yes ... but she still wasn't a 'worker' under the Act. Time to get the wolf at the door to share his sandwiches. *(Edmonds v Lawson, 2000)*

# I SUE YOU!

The King Wu Tut Tut Revue was a burlesque troupe touring England in the early 1920s. They were paid so little that the chorus girls had no choice but to ply an older trade as well. The secretary of the Actors' Association, Mr Lugg, found this situation unbearable. Somehow he had to save the girls. He could have gone for the juggler; instead he persuaded local theatre companies to cancel their contracts with the troupe, so that they all wound up stranded in Maidenhead. The manager was undaunted. He leered, twirled his moustache, and sued Lugg for inducing breach of contract.

The Chancery Division decided that Lugg had done the right thing, and Arnold had to pay his girls a living wage. *(Brimelow v Casson, 1924)*

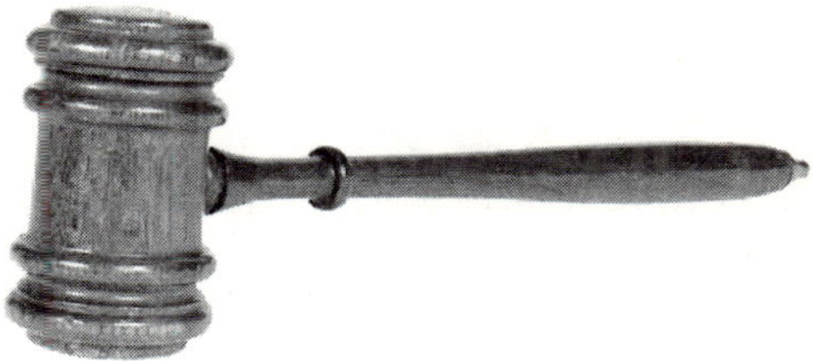

# WE ARE FAMILY until we get into court...

Who got up on the wrong side of the floor this morning? Hats off to Caron and Justin Taylor, who recovered £2,000 damages from their hotel after the four-poster bed they were lying on collapsed on their wedding night. *(Times, 19 May 2006)*

# I SUE YOU!

Can't live with them, can't shoot them in the street without somebody trying to interfere. Cindy Lourcey was delivering post when she saw Mr and Mrs Scarlett fighting in the street. She tried to make them see sense. Instead, Charles Scarlett drew a pistol. He shot his wife in the head, then he made sure Lourcey was watching when he shot himself. Lourcey is suing his estate for intentional infliction of emotional distress. *(Lourcey v Scarlett, Sup Ct Tenn, 2004)*

Dave Piscitelli was having marital trouble, so he looked for a fortune-teller in Yellow Pages. He entered the 'pyramid-shaped Temple of Hope and Knowledge' in Woolworths in Atlantic City, where 'Sole Mio Balaam Nicola' asked for $400 'under the desk' to remove a curse. If he didn't leave his wife, Dave was told, he'd be attacked by snakes. Twenty years later he had no wife, no snakes, and a nervous breakdown. He sued for the $600,000 he'd paid to Nicola's 'gypsy scam' over the years. Sadly – due to unforeseen circumstances? – Nicola had gone bankrupt. *(Piscitelli v Nicola, 2003) )*

H. Beatty Chadwick from Philadelphia has so far spent 11 years in jail for contempt of court, because he is refusing to tell his ex-wife what he's done with $2.5 million he's allegedly hidden in off-shore bank accounts. If he'd stolen the money, he'd have been free after 7 years. *(Times, 24 March 2006)*

## WE ARE FAMILY until we get into court...

A happily married couple found themselves being divorced by a Cairo court because the 70 year-old wife, Nawal El Saadawi, an outspoken feminist, was no longer a Muslim. But an Islamist lawyer's petition to split them up failed; only the state prosecutor can bring such cases, not individuals.

*(DOL International News, 31 July 2001)*

# I SUE YOU!

In a divorce, the wife often gets custody of the family money. Not in Egypt. Under Egyptian divorce law, a husband can serve an obedience order on his wife, forcing her to go back to him or forfeit her right to his financial support. Mona Hanan's husband had been giving her one Egyptian pound (about 10p) a day for her and their 8 year-old son to live on, so they ran for it. She objected to her husband's obedience notice ... and got nothing at all. *(Guardian, 30 November 2004)*

Linda Riss was terrorised by Burton Pugach,

a 'miscreant masquerading as a respectable attorney'. 'If I can't have you, no one else will have you,' he said, 'and when I get through with you, no one else will want you.' In June 1959 she became engaged to another man, so Pugach hired thugs to throw lye in her face. Linda was blinded in one eye, nearly blinded in the other and her face was permanently scarred. Pugach served 14 years in prison and on his release, proposed marriage to Linda Riss. They were married in November 1974. *(Riss v New York, 1968)*

By 1996 Pugach had been having an extra-marital affair with a nurse for 5 years. He threatened her too. 'It's 1959 all over again,' she told police. Still blindly in love, his wife stood character witness on his behalf in court and they sued the nurse together for malicious prosecution. *(Pugach v Borja, 1998)*

So many billionaires, so little time. Orly Hadida proudly runs the world's most expensive matchmaking business. Why drive a Toyota all your life when you could be in a Rolls, she says, and charges $125,000 for 3 years of introductions. Anne Majerik, a 60 year-old widow, has sued her for failing to find her the billionaire of her dreams. One 'international banker' turned out to be an interpreter who worked in a bank. Majerik has won $2 million. *(Times, 1 June 2006)*

# I SUE YOU!

Some children only have distant relatives. Their parents are the kind who take them aside and leave them there. Five 'orphans of the living' aged 2 – 8 years successfully sued in 1978 for emotional and psychological injury caused by their useless mothers. *(Burnette v Wahl, Oregon, 1978)*

'Why don't we try some new positions tonight, dear?' 'No problem, you can stand here at the sink and I'll lie on the sofa.' In Oklahoma five children sued a wealthy widow for luring their father away after 18 years of marriage. The Court of Appeal held that it wasn't the widow's fault if their father was bored at home. *(Nash v Baker, 1974)*

# I SUE YOU!

Damien Bairi was fed up with his North African name. He knew that if he had a posher name he might get a better job and a better life. Why not take the name of France's most swashbuckling hero, D'Artagnan? The Company of Musketeers in Paris sued to try to stop him from taking the fictional character's name, and failed. *(Times, 6 March 2006)*

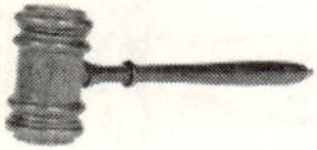

Woody Allen blames his traumatic childhood on being breast-fed from falsies; at least his mother might have been heard in court. UK Judge Philpot let a suspected thief go free because he found a witness too disruptive. She was breastfeeding her 13 week-old baby. *(R v Demelza Pilfold, 4 October 1999)*

In 1908 a Cambridge undergraduate with a taste for fancy waistcoats ran up tailoring bills of over £145. The tailor sued for the debt. The young man claimed that as he was under 21 and the waistcoats were not 'necessaries', he didn't have to pay under the law as it then stood. His father helpfully chipped in that the boy did indeed have 11 perfectly fine waistcoats. Case dismissed. *(Nash v Inman, 1908)*

Tallulah Bankhead defined a liberal education as being able to read the Bible and Shakespeare and shoot dice. In 1971 the parents of a 17 year-old girl sued Chicago University, Illinois for letting her hang around with criminals and be 'seduced' into sex and drugs, thereby causing her not to want to go home to mummy and daddy any more. It was found that the university had no duty to regulate her social life, or her relationship with her parents. *(Hegel v Langsam, 1971)*

An uncle promised to pay his nephew $5,000 if he kept away from 'drinking liquor, using tobacco, swearing and playing cards or billiards for money' until he was 21. A tall order, but the nephew did it. Meanwhile, the uncle died. The young man pursued the executor for his promised cash like an unpaid legal bill all the way to the New York Appeal Court, where he won his case. *(Hamer v Sidway, 1891)*

# THIRSTING FOR JUSTICE

Louis XV is reputed to have said, "What is life without coffee? In fact, what is it with coffee?" In 1992 Stella Liebeck found the answer: it's a pain and she knew where. She bought a cup of coffee from a drive-through McDonald's. She was adding sugar to it in her grandson's parked car when the coffee spilled into her lap leaving her with third-degree burns over her perineum, buttocks and groin. She was in hospital for

8 days and had to have several skin grafts. McDonald's offered her $800 compensation. A jury in Albuquerque, New Mexico upped that to almost $2.9 million damages, reduced on appeal. She eventually settled for an undisclosed sum around $600,000.

*(Stella Liebeck v McDonald's Corp, 1992)*

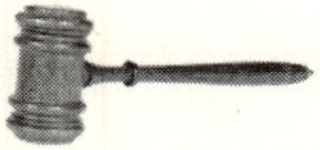

To a lawyer, takeaway coffee must have the delicious smell of pure roast money. In 1998 Angelina McMahon was pouring coffee from one Styrofoam cup into another, so that her husband could also drink some whist driving. She got the lot in her lap, and as she didn't enjoy the resulting second-degree burns, she sued the coffee machine company. But the company claimed that the coffee machine had done exactly what it was supposed to do. Coffee had to be hot, it said. (Isn't that how you distinguish it from what you pour out of your wellies?)

The court agreed; the company did not have to pay. *(McMahon v Bunn-O-Matic, 1998)*

In the Wellmeadow café in Paisley, Scotland, in August 1928, two ladies ordered their tea, and thereby changed the course of legal history. Mrs May Donoghue asked for an 'ice cream float', for which her friend paid. The café owner poured ginger beer over her ice cream, and when he topped her up, Mrs

Donoghue watched a decomposed snail float out of the ginger beer bottle. She took to her bed, then took the ginger beer manufacturers all the way to the House of Lords. In 1942, with enemy bombers whizzing overhead, the most senior court in the United Kingdom took time to consider her and her decomposed snail. It was found that even though she had not paid for the drink herself, the ginger beer company owed her a 'duty of care', and she won her case. *(Donoghue v Stevenson, 1942)*

# I SUE YOU!

It was a wet day, the church picnic group had nowhere to go, and so the Glasgow Corporation kindly offered them the use of a tearoom. When it was time for tea, the urn was being carried past some children buying ice creams. It spilled, scalding some children. Were the kind hosts liable? The House of Lords must have acquired a taste for Scottish cases of this magnitude. It decided they were not. *(Glasgow Corporation v Muir, 1943)*

In 1977 Daisy Ellington bought a bottle of Coca-Cola and had a swig or two of it while she was having her hair done. Later, when she had put her glasses back on, she saw what she thought was a worm inside the bottle. She threw up for a month, became dehydrated and caught a kidney infection. The 'worm' turned out to have been a piece of 'Good-n-Plenty' candy, consisting mostly of sugar. Ellington sued the Coca-Cola bottling company anyway, and lost. *(Ellington v Coca-Cola Bottling Co, Tulsa, Inc, 1986)*

Sione Olive, 26, stood trial in a San Mateo, California court for driving under the influence of kava tea. He passed a breathalyzer test and might have gone free had he not told the police about the 23 cups of kava tea he'd drunk. Kava tea is used for stress relief and 'promoting a state of relaxed unconcern'.

*(Associated Press, 21 August, 2001)*

In 2005 student binge-drinking was becoming a problem around the University of Wisconsin-Madison, so local bars agreed to stop having special offers on Friday and Saturday nights. The students sued them, alleging a price-fixing (anti-trust) conspiracy. A Wisconsin judge threw the case out, and the bars reinstated their discounts anyway. *(Associated Press, 11 May 2005)*

It only takes one drink to get drunk; the trick is to remember whether it's the thirteenth or fourteenth one that does it. The party was going well until Dobler, who was under 21, started swinging a hammer around. Nichols got in the way, and sued the host. Is violence a foreseeable result when you combine youngsters with large amounts of alcohol? The Michigan Appeals Court said yes, it is. *(Nichols v Dobler, 2002)*

As Voltaire said, common sense is not so common. Four friends went shooting one night in Morgan County and had a few beers on the way. Woods fell asleep and the others decided to play a trick on him. On arrival, they planned to load up one bullet each, fire their guns into the ground close to Woods, shout 'it's time to die' and then fire at him. When the plan was put into action two of the guns went off with a click, but the third fired, with fatal consequences. Woods' estate successfully sued the man who had thought up the prank. *(Woods v Cole, 1998)*

# I SUE YOU!

Benjamin Franklin saw beer as proof that God loves us and wants us to be happy. Dan Shelton wants to sell Seriously Bad Elf Beer. His label shows a naughty elf firing a catapult at the Christmas baubles on Santa's sleigh. Connecticut state law forbids the use of images on alcohol that might lead children astray. Shelton claims that these restrictions violate his constitutional rights to free speech and religion. *(The Post-Crescent, Appleton, Wisconsin, December 2005)*

Paul Borland from Queensland, Australia, got drunk for the last time in 1995. He crashed on the couch at his friend's house, very drunk, woke up and decided to jump into the canal from the fence around the back deck. He landed in shallow water and was horribly crippled. Paul admitted that he was an idiot. He was famous for it. If the owners had put up a warning sign or even barbed wire, he'd still have jumped. Nevertheless, the house owners, who weren't even there at the time, were held 70% liable for his injuries.

Boone and Martinez were old enemies. Boone had beaten Martinez up years ago, and Martinez hadn't forgotten. He had a few rounds of drink one day, and reckoned it was time for revenge, so he thumped Boone from behind with a beer mug. Was the bar to blame for failing to keep Boone safe from attack? The Minnesota Supreme Court said no. *(Boone v Martinez, 1997)*

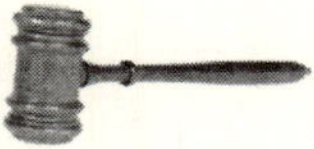

## THIRSTING FOR JUSTICE

The only bar in town was like a pigsty with a jukebox, except that there was no jukebox, so the lads went to the car park to fight. When the police broke it up, they retired to a local store where one of them was shot dead. His heirs sued the store for failing to provide a safe environment. The Mississippi Supreme Court held that the victim had come into the store as part of the fight, at his own risk. *(Titus v Williams, 2003)*

'Doctor, doctor, can I have a second opinion?' 'Sure you can, come back tomorrow.' A man walked into casualty, vomiting. The doctor sent him away, telling him to go and see his GP the next morning. Five hours later the man died of arsenic poisoning. Even though he hadn't bothered to examine him, the doctor was not held to have been liable, as the man would have died anyway. *(Barnett v Chelsea and Kensington Hospital, 1969)*

Barbie went into the library and shouted, 'I want some ribs and some fries please!' The librarian said, 'Do you mind! This is a library!' So Barbie whispered, 'Sorree, I want some ribs and some fries please.' The Canadian Supreme Court has thrown out Mattel Inc.'s trademark suit against a Montreal chain of barbecue restaurants called Barbie's Resto Bar because nobody in their right mind could confuse a Barbie doll with a hearty plate of barbecued food. *(Reuters, 2 June 2006)*

# EVERYBODY NEEDS GOOD...

Maria Muresan was ordered to do 20 days' community service in Transylvania for airing her differences. To annoy her husband she had taken to singing and running around their block of flats naked. The singing was what really got on the neighbours' nerves, but when police told them that singing wasn't an offence but nudity was, they complained about that instead. This in spite of the fact that most of the men had felt that she 'brightened the place up'. *(Ananova.com, 2006)*

Drink had been consumed. Mr Lane was chatting in the street when his neighbour, Mrs Holloway, yelled from a window, 'You bloody lot!' Mr Lane wittily replied, 'Shut up, you monkey-faced tart', at which point her husband offered to 'see the plaintiff on his own'. Mr Lane got his retaliation in first by punching Holloway's shoulder, then Holloway gave him a thump in the eye requiring 19 stitches. Lane sued for assault and battery and won. UK brawlers must accept the risk of proportionate blows, but not 'savagery out of all proportion'. (Lane v Holloway, 1968)

There should be music everywhere, except next door. In 1893, the music lessons next door were driving the defendant up the wall. To get his own back, he started blowing whistles and hammering on tin trays. The music teacher won an injunction to shut him up. *(Christie v Davey, 1893)*

A member of a Sex Pistols' 'tribute band' had his drums confiscated after neighbours complained about the noise. Joe Feeley, who had a particular taste for 'Anarchy in the UK' at three in the morning, didn't even hear the bailiffs knocking at his door when they came to relieve him of £3,000 worth of equipment. *(Manchester Online, 29 April 2004)*

Camden, council let two flats next to each other, and left one without a lock on the door. Thieves strolled in, tunnelled next door and helped themselves. The council was not liable to the owners of the locked flat; it wasn't their fault that the thieves were so devoted to their work. *(Perl v Camden, 1984)*

A lodger in a leased shop told the landlord that he could smell gas. The landlord's advice? Light a match. They were held jointly liable for the damage. *(Brooke v Bool, 1928)*

Neighbours are suing Shannon Peterson in Denver, Colorado for 'reckless and negligent use of her bathtub'. Marvin and Goldie Smith (83 and 78 years old respectively) claim that her daily bath at 5am shakes their water pipes so noisily that they can't sleep, and could she do it later please. *(Denver Post, March 2006)*

Raymond Hugh McNealy exposed his buttocks to a neighbour to convey his compliments during an argument. A Maryland Circuit Court judge ruled that mooning is 'disgusting' but it's not indecent exposure. Had the defendant been on trial for 'being a jerk', the judge said he might have decided otherwise. *(Washington Post, January 2006)*

A 27 year-old woman has been banned from answering her front door wearing only her underwear. Neighbours in

Lanarkshire, Scotland, claimed that Caroline Shepherd was just doing it to annoy them, and that it was unfair on the paperboy. *(Sunday Times, 6 March 2005)*

In The Million Pound Tree case, the House of Lords awarded £1 million to the owners of Delaware Mansions in Maida Vale because the roots of a single plane tree were damaging the mansion block's foundations. *(Delaware Mansions v Lord Mayor & Citizens of Westminster, 2001)*

William Cochrane Jr hates weddings. His neighbour Richard A Demonbreun rents out his historic home for weddings and has sued Mr Cochrane for starting his lawnmower at the very moment a bride and groom exchanged their vows. Any chance they'll all live happily ever after? *(Nashville City Paper, June 2005)*

# I SUE YOU!

Blood is thicker than water, and a lot harder to get out of a shirt. From 1863 to 1891 the Kentucky families Hatfield and McCoy loathed each other. Things didn't improve when Roseanna McCoy ran off to live with Jonse Hatfield. Now the families are fighting again, this time over access to a McCoy cemetery. The cemetery contains the graves of three McCoys slaughtered in 1882. John Vance (a Hatfield) claims the graves are part of Hatfield heritage too. Luckily now it's only access they want; they're not trying to put anybody in there. (Washington Times, 2002 & 'An American Vendetta' by TC Crawford, 1889)

# ADVICE ON THE ASPIRIN BOTTLE: TAKE TWO AND KEEP AWAY FROM CHILDREN...

Brian Dailey, aged 5 years and 9 months, was visiting two old ladies in their garden on 16 July 1951. One of them was about to sit down on a chair when he pulled it out from under her. She broke her hip and successfully sued him in the Washington Supreme Court for $11,000. *(Garratt v Dailey, 1955)*

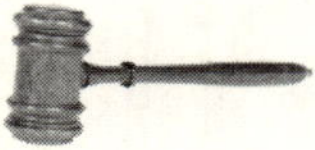

Workmen digging a hole in Russell Road, Edinburgh, wanted their tea break, so they put a tent over the hole and surrounded the tent with paraffin lamps. An 8 year-old boy helped himself to one of the lamps and went exploring inside the tent. He dropped the lamp, tripped over it and the hole blew up. The House of Lords said that boy's act was entirely foreseeable. The workmen's employers were responsible for his burns. *(Hughes v Lord Advocate, 1963)*

Help, I need a lawyer, call the nearest golf course! James, aged 11, was demonstrating his swing to 9 year-old Judith when he walloped her around the jaw by mistake. Judith's father sued the boy's father for foolishly leaving the golf club lying in the back yard, and lost. *(Lubitz v Wells, 1955)*

A driver parked his horse-drawn van in a street near three schools. A child threw a stone at the horse, which bolted. A police officer stepped in to stop the horse. The horse driver was liable for the policeman's injuries regardless of the young bowler's contribution. *(Haynes v Harwood, KB, 1935)*

# ADVICE ON THE ASPIRIN BOTTLE: TAKE TWO AND KEEP AWAY FROM CHILDREN...

The defendants left their coach in a car park with the petrol tank drained. A small boy chucked a lighted match into the tank, injuring a lad on some wasteland nearby. The court decided that boys will be boys and they will throw matches, but somebody else had removed the petrol cap. That was unforeseeable and beyond the defendants' control, which meant that they were not liable. *(Perry v Kendricks Transport Ltd, 1956)*

And when boys grow up ... Tim Bargfrede, 18, is suing the owners of two multi-storey car parks in Orlando, Florida for forgetting to fence their roofs. Tim's friend had managed to jump more than 20 feet from one car park roof to the other, but Tim had fallen 80 feet and fractured his shoulder. 'I just didn't make it,' he said. *(St Petersburg Times, 1 January 2005)*

# SUGAR AND SPICE

Sara Beckman's parents threatened to slap an injunction on the organisers of a state spelling bee after she came only third in the county contest. The eighth grader had correctly spelled 'discernible' and the judges didn't notice that they had the wrong answer on their sheet. The parties managed to settle their discernible differences out of court. *(Kansas City Star, 15 February 2006)*

# I SUE YOU!

Where there's smoke, there's cooking, and when young people are involved it's often cordon noir. Two Colorado teenagers were so proud of their excellent, home-baked cookies, they left some outside a neighbour's door with a heart-shaped card. When Wanita Renea Young saw their unfamiliar shadows moving outside her front door after ten o'clock in the evening, she had an anxiety attack which landed her in hospital. She won $930 in medical costs. *(Denver Post, September 2005)*

The best way to double your money is to fold it up and put it back in your pocket. It's absolutely not to go to court. Peer Larson, 17, discovered this simple maths the hard way when he tried to sue the Wisconsin superintendent of public instruction to get summer homework done away with. He claimed that on top of a 180-day school year, his summer maths project was really too much. Complaint dismissed. *(Pittsburgh Tribune-Review, February 2005)*

# I SUE YOU!

A boy at Milton High School, Massachusetts, has filed a complaint that his school unfairly favours girls. 'If you sit down, follow orders and listen to what they say, you'll do well and get good grades,' says his father, representing him, 'Men naturally rebel against this.' *(Boston Globe, February 2006)*

# DOG EAT DOG

Jeff Delott, a New York attorney, won his client a five-figure settlement in a cat custody case. The judge clearly used criteria similar to those applied in child custody cases. He decided in favour of what, all things considered, and bearing in mind the stress and heartbreak felt by all concerned, was ultimately in the best interests of the lawyers. *(CNN.com, 7 January 2004)*

# I SUE YOU!

It's been said that a horse, like Cary Grant, lends romance to any venture.

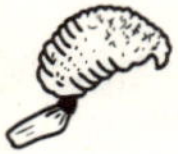

Miss Turnage was sitting in the front row of the circus enjoying the dancing horses until one stopped in front of her, lifted its tail and dumped a pile of rose manure in her lap. Everyone thought it hilarious except Miss Turnage who sued for 'embarrassment, mortification and mental pain and suffering'. (Turnage v Christy Brothers Circus, 1928)

## DOG EAT DOG

When does a cow go cheap? When her owner and buyer both think she's infertile. A cow was sold for $80 on the basis that she couldn't calve. Never had and never could, no sir. Between closing the deal and handing her over, the owner discovered happy news: she was expecting the patter of tiny hooves. That made her worth up to $1,000. The owner refused to part with her, saying the sale was all a mistake. The Supreme Court of Michigan agreed with him. *(Sherwood v Walker, 1887)*

Mary Lee Sowder is suing Petsmart for $100,000 because she slipped in the shop on some doggie drool. She claims she should have had some sort of warning. Pet stores may contain pets? *(Wall Street Journal, 20 June 2001)*

Diane Marcotte, 50, thought she was in enough trouble. She'd been caught driving while drunk. Then the police smelt alcohol on the breath of her 5 month-old Chihuahua puppy too.

He'd lapped up some red wine she'd spilt while driving. End result: $100 fine, and a new home for the pup. *(Associated Press, 23 May 2006)*

Let the buyer beware, especially when buying a killer dog. Lancaster County Prison owned Diesel, a 134 lb Rottweiler, for 14 months, and trained him in prisoner control. Diesel was so happy in his work that he bit prison guards on five separate occasions. The prison gave him

away to Guard Dogs Unlimited, saying that he was 'very well trained', he'd just 'nipped' once when his handler was breaking up a dog fight. Within 2 months Diesel had mauled his new owner as well as an employee. They sued the prison and won $1.5 million each.
*(Reynolds v Lancaster County Prison, 1999)*

In March 2005, 13 year-old Kyle DeVito was walking the family dog when the dog was killed by 'stray voltage' from an old NStar Electric lamppost site. The family are suing NStar. Their first claim was for $1.4 million, the equivalent of the last annual bonus of NStar's chief executive. Now they've selflessly reduced their claim to $740,000, the amount of NStar's chief exec's annual salary. 'We didn't want to appear greedy,' said the family's lawyer, 'We've tried to come up with an offer that had some poetry to it.' *(Boston Globe, March 2005)*

# I SUE YOU!

Richard Espinosa gets panic attacks, so his 'assistance dog' Kimba, a Labrador mix, goes everywhere with him. LC is the local library cat. He usually sits on a pillow near the library door. On 16 November 2000 LC attacked Kimba, and the dog's injuries cost $46.49 in vet's bills. Mr Espinosa, who represented himself, lost his claim for $1.5 million in damages from the City of Escondido. (NBC San Diego.com, 2004)

# DOCTOR, DOCTOR

In October 1962 Ned Searight went to an eye clinic in Newark where they treated his left eye with a radium electric beam. After the operation 'someone' started talking to him inside his brain, so he sued for $12 million. The court debated lengthily about whether a chain of paper clips pinned to Mr Searight's trouser leg might have 'grounded' static electricity and silenced the voice, but in the end they decided they didn't have to decide. He had not filed his suit until 1976 and was out of time. The voice should have spoken up sooner. (Searight v New Jersey, 1976)

A Minnesota woman went to the doctor with ear trouble. The doctor was very brave about her illness and they agreed to an operation on her right ear. In theatre, the doctor found that the right ear did not need surgery after all but her left one did. He put that right and all went well, until the patient sued him for 'battery'.

She had not consented to interference with her left ear. The doctor could hardly believe his own ears when she was awarded $14,322.50 damages, reduced on appeal to $39. *(Mohr v Williams, SC Minnesota, 1905)*

On a dark and stormy night in 1881, Dr de May was called out to help Mrs Roberts give birth. The doctor was exhausted and not feeling well, so he persuaded his friend

Scattergood to accompany him. Scattergood's job was to carry de May's lantern, umbrella and other technical items. When Mrs Roberts discovered that Scattergood was completely unencumbered by medical qualifications, she sued them both and won damages for breach of privacy at such a 'sacred' time.

*(De May v Roberts, SC Michigan, 1881)*

A one-legged woman won damages when she discovered that she had been undressed and touched up by a doctor not of medicine but of theology. *(Commonwealth v Gregory, 1938)*

Mrs Weiland cricked her neck because of a carpet maker's negligence and couldn't adjust her bifocals. How was she to get home? Would she be safe on public transport? Her son agreed to drive her home but while she was making her way to his office, Mrs Weiland fell down some steps. The carpet manufacturer was held liable for all her injuries. *(Weiland v Cyril Lord Carpets Ltd., 1969)*

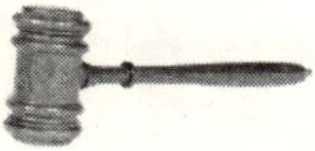

Apart from bad luck, Laura Lee Medley does not seem to have any luck at all. First, she says, she was paralysed in a drink-driving accident. She then sued in four Californian cities for injuries sustained while trying to navigate her wheelchair. Worst of all, when the police closed in on her suspecting her of fraud, she was spotted sprinting out of the hospital. A miracle? She's facing charges of filing false documents, attempted grand theft and insurance fraud. *(Yahoo News, 12 May 2006)*

Dermatitis is pants. It's official. Mr Grant bought some new underwear, developed dermatitis, and sued the manufacturers of the underwear. Was he being rash? No. 'Excessive sulphites' had been left in the fabric and the manufacturers had to compensate him. *(Grant v Australian Knitting Mills, 1936)*

The defendants left a hammer on the pavement to warn people there was a hole. The plaintiff, a blind man, tripped over the hammer and won damages. The defendants should not have been blind to the needs of the blind. (Haley v LEB, 1965)

# GOOD SPORTS

When you win, nothing hurts. When you don't... Lee was bench-pressing a 565-pound bar in a weight-lifting competition when it slipped and landed on him. He blamed the 'spotters' for not catching the bar and saving him. The New York Supreme Court held that he'd taken the risk on himself by entering the competition. *(Lee v Maloney, 1999)*

A cricket ball soared out of the ground and hit a woman standing in the road. The ball had travelled a hundred yards. The crowd erupted: there'd been only six shots like it in the previous thirty years. Sadly, blood erupted from the woman's head too. She sued and lost. The batsman deserved a medal, not a trip to the Court of Appeal. *(Bolton v Stone, 1951)*

Gil-de-Rebollo was looking forward to a quiet basketball game between the Miami Heat and the Atlanta Hawks in Puerto Rico when the Heat's mascot 'Burnie' hauled her out of her front seat to take part in a stunt. She fought back, fell over and was manhandled onto the court. She sued for minor bruises and emotional distress and won $50,000 damages. *(Gil-de-Rebollo v Miami Heat Assn. Inc, 1998)*

'Mummy, can I go swimming?' 'No, darling, the water's too rough.' 'But daddy's swimming!' 'Yes love, but he has life insurance.' Earnsberger was a regular at an Ohio swimming club. The club adjusted the diving board to make it less springy and had to compensate Earnsberger when he found it less giving than he was used to and ruptured a tendon in his knee. *(Earnsberger v Griffiths Park Swim Club, 2002)*

At St Augustine's Golf Club people regularly overshot the thirteenth. In 1922 a chap was driving past when a golf ball hit him on the head. It's a funny old game, but the judge wasn't laughing. The club was liable in public nuisance. *(Castle v St Augustine's links, 1922)*

Some of us would rather watch Astroturf grow than sit through a game of baseball, but Reider loved it. She was about to buy a ticket for a game at McNeese State University when a ball sailed out of the ground into her face. A jury awarded her $485,000. Ball park owners can't be liable for every rogue ball, but they should at least let people buy their tickets without fear of injury. *(State of Louisiana v Reider, 2005)*

Police raided a Scottish golf club and took away an illegal fruit machine. An anonymous verse arrived on the club notice board: 'but he who gave the game away, may he byrne in hell and rue the day.' Club member Mr Byrne sued the golf club for defamation: would he stoop so low as to grass to the police? The court decided he had not been defamed, as no right-thinking member of society would see the verse as an insult. *(Byrne v Deane, 1937)*

'Two, four, six, eight, we don't jump because a nail might break.' Cheerleaders in Catasauqua,

Pennsylvania, fought a ban on dangerous cheerleading stunts and won. The Colonial League had banned some of their mounts and tumbles as 'dangerous and unnecessary'. The girls protested that cheerleading was a sport, not just entertainment, and proved in court that they're as tough as anybody. *(Associated Press, 19 October 2001)*

# LOOK BOTH WAYS BEFORE SUING

A drunk is somebody who goes into a bar optimistically and comes out misty optically. Brian Lee Tarver left an Exxon petrol station in Tennessee the same way. He'd just bought $3 of petrol and went on to have a head-on crash. His victims won the right to sue Exxon for selling him that spoonful of petrol. *(Knoxville News-Sentinel, September 2005)*

# I SUE YOU!

Sometimes when we park the car there can be an invigorating walk to the pavement. John Leat didn't make that mistake. When he went to the dentist, he parked his Mercedes-Benz so close to Louise Hamilton's flat that she could hardly get to her front door. Mrs Hamilton, a pensioner, leant on the car to write him a note. Mr Leat won over £1,000 for repairs to the bonnet. *(Times, 2 March 2006)*

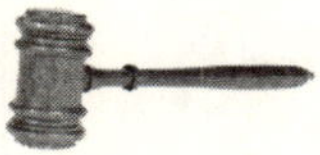

# LOOK BOTH WAYS BEFORE SUING

Some cars have three speeds: fast, faster and 'Guilty, your Honour'. Lorry driver Charles Glendinning, 56, has been cleared of warning other motorists about a speed trap on the A303 in Somerset. He was convicted of obstructing the police, but in May 2006 the House of Lords upheld his appeal. *(Times, 9 May 2006)*

On the way to see George VI's coronation lights, the party developed a thirst and found themselves enjoying several public houses on the way. One passenger decided that the driver was too drunk to take them any further and got out of the car. The plaintiff stayed put, saying she'd risk an accident. Minutes later the car crashed and the plaintiff was injured. The driver had to pay up. *(Dann v Hamilton, 1939)*

# LOOK BOTH WAYS BEFORE SUING

Witty and Knight had been out drinking when 20 year-old Knight stopped his car to buy cigarettes. He locked his keys inside the car, so he called his father to bring a spare, which the father did. Knight drove on, with Witty still in the car, and had an accident in which Witty was killed. Witty's heirs sued Knight senior for handing over that key. The father was held not responsible; Witty shouldn't have got in the car. *(Coble v Knight, 1998)*

'There is no question that Erma Veith was subject at the time of the accident to an insane delusion...' You're not wrong, Chief Justice Hallows. She thought she was driving on the wrong side of the road because God had taken hold of her steering wheel. She also believed that if she drove fast enough, her car would fly like Batman. She was flying after her car hit the truck all right, but not in the way she expected. A psychiatrist stated that she had suffered an unforeseeable schizophrenic reaction. The court also heard evidence, however, that it wasn't the first time she'd let God drive her around the bend. Her insurance company was liable for the truck driver's injuries after all. *(Breunig v American Family Ins Co, 1970)*

The railroad company had left a mud hole in the road. In January 1919 a car got stuck in it and a man with a wooden leg, Mr Morrow, offered to help. Mr Morrow was tugging with a towrope when his wooden leg got stuck in the mud too, so he grabbed the back of the tow truck. The tow truck began to move and the towrope caught up around B's good leg and broke it. Mr Morrow was rewarded with $9,500 damages, as well as immortality as the hero of 'the peg leg case'. *(Hines v Morrow, 1921)*

Somebody had already pranged Mr Abraham's Rolls when the defendant managed to hit it again, on the same spot. The court held that the second driver did not need to pay for the respray, as the car already needed one. *(Performance Cars v Abraham, 1962)*

A woman sued a driver who ran his car over her legs while she was sunbathing. Where? In a hotel car park. *(Letang v Cooper, 1965)*

The plaintiff was travelling in a horse-drawn coach when a coupling rein broke. Thinking the coach was bound to crash, the plaintiff flung himself out and broke his leg. The coach did not crash after all. In fact everybody else was fine. The coach owner was liable for the plaintiff's injuries anyway. *(Jones v Boyce, 1816)*

Harrison was trying to jump onto a moving train. The guard signalled the driver but managed to give the wrong signal, so the train sped out of the station with the guard pulling at Harrison until they both fell out. Harrison was 80% liable for the guard's injuries. *(Harrison v BRB, 1981)*

A lady was waiting for her train. Another train drew up and a man holding a parcel jumped on while the train was moving. He wobbled, so two guards helped him on. In the commotion, the man's parcel fell onto the rails and exploded. It was a packet of fireworks. At the other end of the platform, several feet away, some scales were knocked over by the blast, and fell on the lady. The railway company was not liable; parcels don't usually explode. *(Palsgraf v Long Island RR Co., 1928)*

# LOOK BOTH WAYS BEFORE SUING

Mr Goddard stepped off the train onto a crowded platform where he slipped and fell on a banana skin. It took the Supreme Judicial Court of Massachusetts to persuade him that anybody could have dropped the banana skin seconds earlier and that the railroad company was not liable.

*(Goddard v Boston & Maine RR Co., 1901)*

Is it safe to walk the streets? San Franciscans were celebrating V-J Day on 14 August 1945. The plaintiff was walking past a hotel when a stuffed armchair landed on her. Nobody could tell the court quite why the armchair had left the hotel – rock groups hadn't been invented yet – so the hotel was held not responsible. *(Larson v St Francis Hotel, 1948)*

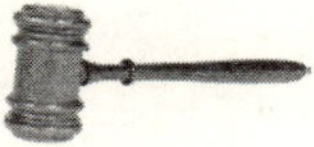

# HOME, SWEET HOME

The only toilet in the house was an outside privy with a dodgy trapdoor in the floor. Not exactly lavish. Mrs Rush knew about the trapdoor but nature's calls couldn't be ignored. She fell about 9 feet through the floor into 'the accumulation below' and had to be helped out up a ladder. New Jersey's Supreme Court held that the trial court's decision – that the landlord was liable – had not fallen between two stools. *(Rush v Commercial Realty, 1929)*

# I SUE YOU!

A New Yorker contracted to buy a house in Nyack village. All the locals knew that the house was a regular haunt of poltergeists. There had been local newspaper articles about it and a walking tour described the house as 'with ghost'. But nobody told the purchaser, who sued for fraudulent misrepresentation. The Supreme Court said he hadn't a ghost of a chance. *(Stambovsky v Ackley, 1991)*

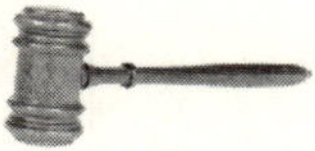

Mr Jarvis booked a fortnight's skiing at Christmas for £63.45. The brochure had said there would be a 'house party', regular afternoon tea and cakes, a fondue party and a yodelling evening. Some people would have paid to skip the yodelling evening, but not Mr Jarvis. In his first week there were 13 other people in the hotel, but the second week he was alone. The afternoon tea consisted of crisps and nutcakes, and the yodeller turned up in his work clothes and only bashed out a few songs. Perhaps most crucially, the 'Alphutte Bar' in the hotel was open for only one evening. Mr Jarvis claimed damages for disappointment, and won. Edmund Davies LJ said his distress was like that of a chap hoping to hear the opera at Glyndebourne whose car failed to turn up. *(Jarvis v Swan Tours, 1973)*

# NO SUCH THING AS BAD PUBLICITY?

The American Italian Defense Association (AIDA) wanted to sue the makers of The Sopranos for infringing the 'individual dignity' of American Italians. They didn't want no fuss, they didn't want no damages, they just wanted to make their point. Clear? It was an offer the judge refused.

*(Los Angeles Times, September 2001)*

Gordon Kaye, from the comedy series Allo, Allo, was hit on the head by an advertising board. While he was recovering quietly in intensive care, the Sunday Sport arrived to flash photograph him. As he didn't mind, the court could find no actionable damage. *(Kaye v Robertson, 1991)*

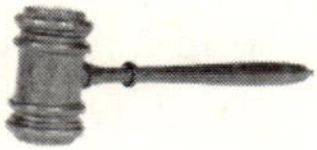

Some guys still think 'harass' is two words. Amaani Lyle, 32, was fired from the Friends'

script-writing team. She was happy to go. She hated all the sexist banter and sued, saying it amounted to sexual harassment. Warner Bros replied that is how writers work, and the show would be less funny without it. The California Supreme Court justices agreed with Warners, 7-nil. *(Associated Press, 20 April 2006)*

'Strewth! What's Harold up to with our Madge?' ran the News of the World headline, beside photographs of the faces of Harold and Madge from Neighbours superimposed on naked bodies entwined in sexual acts. The article discussed a computer game where celebrities' heads are superimposed on porn actors' bodies. The court found it's not libel where readers jump to conclusions from reading nothing but the headlines. *(Charleston v News Group, 1995)*

Some television shows should carry a warning: the show must go off. Austin Aitken saw an episode of 'Fear Factor' in which contestants apparently ate dead rats. He threw up. He became lightheaded and ran into a doorway. Aitken, who says his main concern is not the money, is suing NBC for $25 million. *(Reuters, 7 January 2005)*

Dave 'the Dwarf' Flood has been frozen in ice, has lived in a Dumpster for charity, and has rolled in a giant bowling ball, but what he likes best is being tossed in a bar. In 1989 the state of Florida banned 'dwarf tossing' in which people compete by throwing short people across the bar, sometimes in Velcro suits, so that they stick to the wall. Mr Flood (3 feet 2) sued Governor Jeb Bush (6 feet 4) claiming disability discrimination. The case was tossed out. *(National Law Journal, April 2002)*

Debbie Tay, a topless dancer, had been a regular on Howard Stern's radio show. After she died, Debbie's sister sent some of her ashes to Debbie's friend Hayden so that he could 'honour' his old friend. She then heard that Hayden planned to take the ashes onto Stern's show, and begged him not to do it. Hayden didn't listen. He took the ashes to Stern who mucked about with them and made jokes. The family sued Stern, Hayden and the broadcasting company for intentional infliction of emotional distress. They won. *(Roach v Stern, 1998)*

Shangold and Niederman sent a children's cartoon proposal to Disney in 1994. It was rejected as a 'listless fairy tale'. In 2002, however, Disney published Summerland, which Shangold and Niederman thought they recognised. Wasn't it their proposal, the very same, except that it had a baseball theme, and was well written? So they revised their idea, included the baseball theme, backdated it to 1994 and sued Disney for stealing their work. They might have succeeded except that their '1994' version mentioned Palm Pilots. Which weren't around until 1997. (Law.com, 18 January 2006)

The grass isn't always greener on television. The Sally Jessy Raphael Show was doing a special programme about teenage prostitution. Misty Weber, 15, appeared on it as a 'difficult' teenage runaway but, she claimed, not a prostitute. This was a subtlety that eluded her family who shunned her after the show. The show producers were not liable for defamation.

*(Weber v Multimedia Entertainment Inc., 2000)*

# I SUE YOU!

Death can be nature's way of telling you to call a lawyer. James and Laurie Ann Ryan came back to their hotel room one day to find a blood-covered corpse lying on their bed. Security guards wouldn't let them leave the scene until a paramedic arrived, at which point everyone except the Ryans burst out laughing. It was all a stunt for a pilot MTV show. The Ryans are suing for $10 million each. The show's been pulled. *(Las Vegas Sun, 4 February 2004)*

## NO SUCH THING AS BAD PUBLICITY?

Confession is good for the soul, except on television. During a 1995 recording of the Jenny Jones Show, Scott Amedure admitted he had a crush on Jonathan Schmitz, who was also on the show. Days later Amedure was found murdered and Schmitz is currently serving 25-50 years in prison. Amedure's family sued the show. They initially won $29.3 million, but Michigan's Supreme Court disagreed. Amedure should have saved it for the priest. *(Graves v Warner Bros, 2004)*

# I SUE YOU!

A debtor had won a controversial bankruptcy case. He didn't like the tone of an article about him in New York's Forbes magazine, saying it was 'dripping with disapproval' of his motives. He sued, and lost. It was found that an 'allegation of greed is not defamatory'. *(Wilkow v Forbes, 2001)*

# GOD HELP US

Gerald Mayo had a sympathetic hearing in a US District Court in Pennsylvania when he tried to sue Satan for causing him misery, and generally being responsible for his downfall. The court gently explained that even if Mayo's civil rights had been denied, it did not have jurisdiction over this particular defendant. Nor could they seem to track down his address. *(United States ex rel. Gerald Mayo vs. Satan and his staff, 1971)*

# I SUE YOU!

The Italian Court of Appeal has required Father Enrico Righi to prove that Jesus of Nazareth really existed. Father Righi had denounced author Luigi Cascioli in a parish newsletter for questioning Christ's existence. Cascioli (once a student priest, now a militant atheist) accused Father Righi of 'abuse of popular credulity', an offence under the Italian Penal Code. The Vatican has yet to comment. *(Times, 3 January 2006)*

A clergyman called Woods liked to worship by the sea but found himself in hot water when the local council sued him for trespass. But God moves in mysterious ways. He might even have a sense of humour. The case was thrown out for triviality. *(Llandudno UDC v Woods, 1889)*

The church service in Upper Room Tabernacle Church, Dix Hills, New York was in full swing. People were babbling in tongues and as God's love filled them they would collapse, 'slain in the spirit'. Sophia Reitan was 'slain', fell and broke her arm. 'God loves me,' she cried as she was awarded $80,000. *(Christian Examiner, February 2005)*

Randall Radic, former pastor of First Congregational Church in Ripon, Central Valley, CA is serving 16 months in prison for embezzlement and forgery, after he sold off the church building, land and parsonage. The church directors knew nothing about it until Radic's fiancée was seen driving a new BMW. *(The Record, 31 January 2006)*

When a red gum tree in Western Australia caught fire, the landowner's men chopped it down and left it to burn out. The wind came up and the fire spread to neighbouring land. The Privy Council held that, act of God or not, it should have been all hands to the pumps. *(Hargrave v Goldman, 1967)*

Every Christmas for 40 years Pawtucket, Rhode Island had put up Santa's house, a Christmas tree and a nativity scene during the Christmas season. Daniel Donnelly reckoned this breached the First Amendment's guarantees of freedom of religion and separation of church and state. The Supreme Court said no, it was just a nice thing to do. It also explained that Christmas was about more than looking for a new job after the office party. *(Lynch v Donnelly, 1984)*

Glamour is that indefinable thing about a girl with a huge bosom. Amy Gunderson, 31, was arrested for dressing only in a thong and body paint at the Coney Island Mermaid

Parade. While other mermaids would have rushed to cover up with beads and band aids, Gunderson sued. She claimed that under the First Amendment she had as much right to parade topless as men did. New York City paid her $10,000. *(Boston Globe, 23 April 2003)*

Atheist Roger Florey sued because his children had to sing carols and answer a Christmas quiz at school. The Court of Appeals decided that their religious activities were constitutional as long as the secular aspects of Christmas were taught too. Who's for a school trip to the shopping mall?
*(Florey v Sioux Falls School District, 1980)*

The Ku Klux Klan wanted to celebrate the season of good will by putting up a cross in Capitol Square, Columbus, Ohio. They applied for permission. The square's advisory board refused, citing the First Amendment, but the KKK claimed their constitutional right to freedom of speech all the way to the Supreme Court, and won. *(Capitol Square Review and Advisory Bd v Pinette, 1995)*

A druid who believes he is the reincarnation of King Arthur fought the British government for 14 years for the right to hold druidic festivals at Stonehenge. Peaceful rituals had been held there for about 100 years but Arthur became too popular for his own good. His 1983/4 rituals were swamped by unruly New Age travellers and Arthur was arrested. He appeared in the Salisbury Magistrates' dock in full robes and swore his oath on his 'Sword of Truth', Excalibur. The European Commission of Human Rights was not impressed. His claims for rights of peaceful assembly and of religion were thrown out. (Pendragon v UK, 1998)

# ROGUES AND VAGABONDS

'How come we always catch you on the second floor, Vellino?' 'It's my storey, officer, and I'm sticking to it.' A criminal jumped from a second floor window to avoid being arrested by police. He then sued the police for not making sure he didn't jump. The Court of Appeal decided that it was his own fault.

*(Vellino v Greater Manchester police, 2002)*

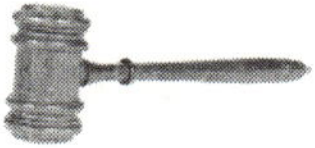

Guns don't kill people – bullets do. Three people were shot dead in New Jersey during a post office robbery, proving Al Capone's dictum that you can get further with a kind word and a gun than with a kind word alone. Their families sued the bullet manufacturers. These were special bullets that opened into razor sharp edges 'to severely rip through and mutilate body parts of the individuals shot by such bullets.' The court held that bullets are bullets, and murder is what they do. *(Leslie v Olin, US, 1997)*

In 1997 a plaintiff gave information to the Northumberland police and successfully sued them when the information wound up in the hands of the very person he'd incriminated. *(Swinney v Chief Constable of Northumberland police, 1997)*

An Alaskan murderer found a new way to add insolence to injury. He sued the manufacturers of his own shotgun for the wages he lost while held in prison and for the legal bills from his trial. No, he didn't win. *(Adkinson v Rossi Arms Company, 1983)*

Two policemen had been murdered in Western Australia and a reward was offered for any help given in tracking their killer. Clarke stepped forward with vital information and claimed the reward. He didn't get it. He was under arrest for the murder at the time. *(R v Clarke, 1927)*

Manners maketh the burglar in Tokyo. After breaking into her apartment and tying her up, 29 year-old Lee Jin-se gave his victim several hours of shoulder massage 'to relax her'. He also relieved her of 210,000 yen in cash and of her banker's card. *(Reuters, 12 May 2006)*

A psychopath was in Mr Rigby's shop. The police fired in CS gas to force him out, and it worked. It also burned down the shop. The police had to compensate: they should have brought fire-fighting equipment before they fired. *(Rigby v Chief Constable of Northamptonshire, 1985)*

'One oil tanker including contents ... said to contain oil' was advertised for sale, lying on an Australian reef. McRae's offer of £285 was accepted, so he set off with his salvage crew to find ... no tanker and no contents. Just like that. The vendor said the contract was void but McRae won his money back plus the salvage costs. *(McRae v Commonwealth Disposals Commission, 1951)*

The managing director and the company chairman of a business in New South Wales didn't get on. The chairman threatened the MD with a hit man. The MD signed $320,000 over to the chairman to buy him out, then claimed the deed was void for having been agreed under duress. But the deed put the company in a better position to get a loan, so wouldn't he have signed it anyway? The Privy Council decided no, and the chairman had to stand in the naughty corner. *(Barton v Armstrong, 1976)*

A 76 year-old man was asleep in his shed guarding his valuables when he heard an intruder. He fired his shotgun through a small hole in the door and wounded a man, who later helped the police solve several other burglaries that night by confessing to them. The burglar sued for breach of section 1 of the Occupiers' Liability Act 1984. Though he had had no business being there at all, he won. *(Revill v Newbery, 1996)*

# I SUE YOU!

Stone walls do not a prison make, nor iron bars a cage, unless you're in prison of course. Drug addicts in UK prisons are suing the Home Office for leaving them to survive their 'cold turkey' without help. They claim this breaches the Human Rights Convention's ban on torture or inhuman or degrading treatment. *(Times, 12 May 2006)*

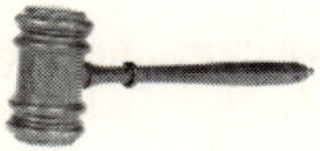

For some people over 50 litigation takes the place of sex. Gunman George Knights, 48, was not going to wait that long. Undaunted by the fact that he deprived 3 police officers of the human right to do their jobs without being shot, he keeps suing the authorities about his prison conditions. First he lost his claim for an extra socket in his cell so that he could use his electric toothbrush and shave at the same time. Next, his claim that staff torches kept him awake at night was thrown out too. Now he reckons his mattress is giving him deep vein thrombosis and if he doesn't get another one, it would constitute 'torture' under the UK Human Rights Act. He has also requested a ground floor cell, as he doesn't care for stairs. *(Times, 13 July 2004)*

Three old ladies wanted to sell their car for cash. A 'Mr Hutchinson' offered them a cheque. When they quibbled, he said he was a respectable businessman and gave them his address. Two of the ladies kept him chatting while the third checked the phone book, and found the name Hutchinson at the address they had been given. They accepted the cheque, and the cheque bounced. Meanwhile the rogue had sold the car on. Usually genuine purchasers will win but in this case the car ended up with a dealer. The judges found for the old ladies. *(Ingram v Little, 1961)*

# I SUE YOU!

Two paintings were sold at a country auction for £840. Weeks later, they sold on for £88,000. Shouldn't the auctioneers have known better? The court thought not. The country firm was like your average GP and should not to be compared to London auction houses (who also make mistakes). Which may be why although Rembrandt left about 300 paintings, about 1,000 of them are in America. *(Luxmoore-May v Messenger May Baverstock, 1990)*

Christine Ryder was clinically fed up and wanted to die. When she asked Kevin Reeves to find a hit man to kill her he agreed, and said it would cost £2,500. She paid up. Nothing happened. When Ryder phoned, upset that she was still alive, she was told the price had risen to £5,000. She paid again, and they agreed on a drive-by shooting in Rochester, Kent on 11 June 2003. Nothing happened. Reeves called this time, saying that he'd had to kill the 'hitman' and give the money to his widow but they could start afresh if she gave him another £10,000. Ryder did so. Reeves did nothing. His excuse this time was that he'd lost the money through bankruptcy but he did promise to kill her himself for another £10,000. They settled on a date. Ryder reached that midnight still breathing because Reeves and his wife were on holiday in Tenerife. But Ryder by now had found a reason to live: she sued Ryder for breach of contract and won. *(Times, 17 January 2006)*

1-905102-10-0

£4.99

HOW TO BE A
BULLSHIT
MANAGER
IN 7 DAYS